Copyright and Publishing Notes

Unless otherwise indicated, all scripture quotations are taken from the
King James Version of the Bible.

Scripture quotations marked **AMP** are taken from *The Amplified Bible, New Testament.* Copyright © The Lockman Foundation 1960, 1962, 1963, 1968, 1971, 1972, 1973, 1975, 1977. Used by permission.

*Greet Me With A Holy Kiss
with 21 Days of Mouth Altering Change – Study Guide*
2nd Edition

ISBN: 0-9664798-1-5

Copyright © 2017 by
Set Free Global Ministries, Inc.
P.O. Box 293042
Lewisville, TX 75029

Printed in the United States of America
All rights reserved under International Copyright Law
Contents and /or cover may not be reproduced in whole or in part in any form without express written consent of the Publisher.

CONTENTS

Dedication	3
Introduction	4
Biblical Perspective on Words	8
Watching Your Words	22
Relationships That Are Affected by Words Spoken	30
Gossiping Is A Kingdom Issue	39
The Mouth Is An Unruly Thing	47
Where Do I Go From Here?	52
21 Days of Mouth Altering – Study Guide	58
Rededication of Your Mouth	110
Entering Into A New Life	111
About The Author	117

DEDICATION

I dedicate this book to my husband, Eric. You are my best friend for life. I believe our best days are ahead. I pray we will continue to be in love, to laugh, and minister together. I still believe, what I've known from the start, that we belong together. I enjoy my life with you.

To my son Chandler, you make Mommy laugh. Thank you for the early morning rides to school as we discuss the Bible and pray in a way that brings joy to us both. You are my little miracle. Yep, I'm going to keep saying it to you and to your Dad that you two are the best things that ever happened to me besides Jesus. You are such a great little character builder and I love you.

I make this promise to you both, to always stay in the presence of God so I can be the best you need me to be.

Love Always,

Deneen

INTRODUCTION

How often do you take the time to examine the words you use in your daily conversations with others? Have you ever taken into consideration the harm that can be inflicted based solely on something you've said? How many times have you let an unkind word slip out of your mouth when talking with a loved one? And, do you ever stop to think whether or not the person you're talking to can handle your particular choice of words?

If you were to carefully examine everything you said to people throughout the day, you may discover that some things you say can be considered abusive and unkind. Child of God, just because you have a right to say something, doesn't make it right to say.

Improper use of your words can cause pain, conflict, strife, confusion and foster discrimination and discord. Plain, everyday words when used in a manner that doesn't take into account the feelings of the person to whom you're speaking, can cause irreparable damage.

I believe that most people, including Christians, have no idea the impact and the power behind the words they speak. We need to understand that the words we speak have the capacity to bring the manifestation of God's glory into our lives, or the ability to bring destruction, lack and pain. Words are spiritual containers and are the substance of what we see in the natural realm.

The Bible gives us instruction on how the words coming out of our mouths should be used, and lets us know through scripture just how important the words are that we speak. Jesus Himself said in ***Matthew 12:37***, ***"For by thy words thou shalt be justified, and by thy words thou shalt be condemned."*** Since the Bible has been given to believers by God as an instruction manual for life, we should take heed to what the Lord shares with us concerning the use of our words. Even if the things you read in the Word of God challenge your flesh, and cause you to re-examine the way you do things, the instructions in the Bible have been given to us for a reason.

This book of the law shall not depart out of thy mouth; but thou shalt meditate therein day and night, that thou mayest observe to do according to all that is written therein: for then thou shalt make thy way prosperous, and then thou shalt have good success. (Joshua 1:8)

God wants you to prosper, and live a life of happiness and abundance. In His infinite wisdom, He knew that the words you chose would be the avenue by which you avail yourself of His many promises. He also knew that they could be the same avenue by which you bring pain, sadness and poverty -- not only in your life, but possibly in the lives of others.

In this book, my objective is to enlighten you as to the power inherent in what you allow to come out of your mouth. By the time you finish the last chapter, you will know beyond a shadow of doubt, that the biblical perspective on the use of words is based on love, compassion and kindness. My prayer is that the anointing power made available to you as a Christian, will compel you to choose and to use your words wisely.

While reading this book, allow the Holy Spirit to minister to you. Allow the Word of God to renew your mind to bring your mouth in line with what thus saith the Lord. Allow the information between these pages to bring you to the place where your prayer can be, *"Let the words of my mouth, and the meditation of my heart, be acceptable in thy sight, O LORD, my strength, and my redeemer." (Psalm 19:4)*

Now, let's take a journey into the world of words!

Chapter One
Biblical Perspective on Words

By reading the book of Genesis, we're able to get a picture of the biblical perspective of words, and their ability to create, transform and bring into existence those things that did not otherwise exist in the physical realm. It was with words that God created the heaven and the earth, trees, earth creatures, the fowl of the air and of course, male and female. It was also with words that He brought the light of day into existence, the dark of night, the sea and herb yielding seed after its kind.

But the question is how did He do all of this? Where did He get the material to create such things? Did God make things with His hands? What did He use? If you follow the scriptures in the first chapter of Genesis closely, you'll see that it was not His hands He used to form the universe. The material He used to create all that we see today, and all that came forth in the beginning, was the faith-filled substance of words.

Deneen Whatley

In the beginning God created the heaven and the earth. And the earth was without form, and void; and darkness was upon the face of the deep. And the Spirit of God moved upon the face of the waters.

And <u>God said</u>, Let there be light…
And <u>God saw</u> the light…
And <u>God said</u>, Let there be a firmament…
And <u>God made</u> the firmament…
And God said, Let the waters under the heaven be gathered together in one place, and let the dry land appear: and it was so.

And <u>God said</u>, Let the earth bring forth grass, the herb yielding seed, and the fruit tree yielding fruit after its kind, whose seed is in itself, upon the earth: and it was so.

And <u>God said</u>, Let there be lights…
And <u>God made</u> two great lights…

And to rule over the day and over the night, and to divide the light from the darkness: and God saw that it was good.

And <u>God said</u>, Let the waters bring forth abundantly the moving creature…

And God made the beast of the earth after his kind… and God saw that it was good.
And <u>God said</u>, Let us make man in our image…

So <u>God created</u> man in his own image…

And <u>God said</u>, Behold, I have given you every herb bearing seed…

And <u>God saw</u> every thing that he had made, and, behold, it was very good.
(Genesis 1:1-4, 6-7, 9, 11, 14, 16, 18, 20, 24-27, 29, 31)

As you can see, God created everything that there was with the words of His mouth. The spoken Word of God is so very powerful, that everything He spoke came into being. And Child of God, He has designed His words to do the same for you. The Word of God spoken out of the mouth of a born-again believer is meant to bring to pass whatever you desire, providing they are spoken in faith.

Now faith is the assurance, (the confirmation, the title deed) of the things (we) hope for, being the proof of things (we) do not see, and the conviction of their reality (faith perceiving as real fact what is not revealed to the senses.) (Hebrews 11:1 Amplified)

Faith is the substance and the manifestation of things hoped for, prayed about and petitioned for. Faith is the material that will produce and bring the unseen thing you hope for into clear view, for everyone to see. The material God uses to bring what He wanted on earth to pass is faith material. As it says in the Amplified Bible, the Word of God is the title deed for your faith. A title deed is proof of ownership. When spoken in faith, the Word of God becomes your title deed, or your proof, that you have what you say. You know of course, that a title deed must be signed in order to make it a legal document. When Jesus died for you, He signed the title deed in His blood. Any situation or circumstance in your life will respond to the Word of God, allowing whatever you've prayed for to travel from the spiritual to the physical, natural realm.

God said, Let Us (Father, Son and Holy Spirit) make mankind in Our image, after Our likeness; and let them have complete authority over the fish of the sea, the birds of the air, the (tame) beasts, and over all the earth, and over every thing that creeps upon the earth. (Genesis 1:26 AMP)

God made us in His image. Then, He gave us authority over every thing in the earth. You didn't have to fight for this or speak it into existence because God gave it to you as a gift. Faith is a gift, freely given. A gift is something you don't have to earn. Someone freely gives it to you. If God's Word says that you were made in His image and His likeness, then the words you speak should also have enough faith material in them to bring themselves to pass.

But, do your words truly have the necessary power in them to bring themselves to pass? If you can't answer this question with confidence, then we need to determine why your confidence level in answering this question is low. As a born-again Christian, your life should be a reflection of the Word of God. If it isn't, you need to find out why. ***Haggai 1:7*** gives us at least one way to determine that, he says to 'consider your ways'.

How do you get your words to manifest themselves from the unseen realm to the physical?

> Jesus said, "*...So is the kingdom of God, as if a man should cast seed into the ground; And should sleep, and rise night and day, and the seed should spring and grow up, he knoweth not how. (Mark 4:26-27)*
>
> *And the Lord said, "If ye had faith as a grain of mustard seed, ye might say unto this sycamine tree, be thou plucked up by the root, and be thou planted in the sea; <u>and it should obey you.</u>" (Luke 17:6)*

Faith, which is equal to the Word of God, is the necessary seed to plant in your heart for a harvest of God's promises to be made manifest. Your soil is your heart, and the Bible tells us in *Proverbs 4:23, to "Keep thy heart with all diligence; for out of it flows the issues of life."* The success of your harvest depends on how well you cultivate the seed you have planted. If a man plants good Word seed in the ground of his heart, he will reap a harvest of blessings. However, you have to continue to cultivate the words you've spoken, and don't allow the weeds of corrupt communication or negative words to creep up and uproot the seed you've planted. Once your heart is contaminated with bad seed, the ground must be pruned. You might say, "Well, I don't know good anointed words, let alone words filled with faith." I'm here to tell you that all you need to do to find these words is open your Bible.

As I said earlier, the Word of God is your manual for life. Whatever your situation or circumstance may be, there's an answer for you in the Word of God. Your next step is to put the words in your ears as you hear it preached, keep the Word before your eyes as you read your Bible daily, and keep the Word of God coming out of your mouth as you confess and mediate upon the scriptures. That's how you get it into your heart. The Word of God must be in these three places---your mouth, your ears and your heart---in order for you to have manifestation of the things you've said. Your mouth is the entrance and exit to your heart, or your spirit.

If you are believing God for healing, what do you do to manifest that healing? Faith alone without works is dead. *(James 2:17)* First of all, you need a concordance so you can locate the necessary scriptures to stand on. Secondly, you will have to meditate on each scripture. Next, confess your healing out loud three or more times a day, putting it in your mouth, in your ears and in your heart. As you repeat each scripture, believe you've received your healing. This needs to be done daily, until your healing is manifested in the natural. The world says, "seeing is believing," but the Word says "believe and you will see." *(Mark 11:24).* That which you don't see is what you should believe you already have. Your goal is to say it and see it. Please don't allow the bondage of this world's way of seeing things to block your manifestation.

Operating in faith is nothing new. You use faith on a day-to-day basis more than you will ever know. Let's look at some examples of how you usually put action to your faith. You get up each morning and prepare yourself for work. After you've dressed, you go outside to get into your car. Granted, you have no idea that your job will be there when you arrive. But, if you didn't have faith that your job would be there, you would not have gotten up and prepared yourself to go. Better yet, when you got into your car and turned the key, did you have any idea that it would start? These are perfect examples of operating in faith and believing for desired results.

Imagine yourself as one who always said you were going to attend college and become a doctor. You did everything you had to do to prepare yourself for that eventuality. You finished high school, received a Bachelor's degree in Biology, took pre-med courses, and received your graduate degree before becoming exactly what you said you would become. When you speak the words of God in faith, they have enough power to bring themselves to pass. Remember, every time you speak something, your words are supposed to have enough power in them to come to pass. There is a way however, that you can block up the very blessing you desire from ever manifesting in your life. The Bible says, ***"Out of the same mouth comes forth blessing and cursing. These things, my brethen, ought not to be so. Does a fountain send forth (simultaneously) from the same opening fresh water and bitter?" (James 3:10-11 AMP)***

By speaking negative words filled with doubt and unbelief you will stop your harvest before it can spring forth. Say for instance, you didn't accomplish a particular desire you had previously spoken about, such as becoming a doctor. Why? Because you started speaking the opposite of what you believed. "I can't do this. School is too hard. I won't even make it into college, because I can't make it out of high school. I'm not smart enough." Then, you started confessing that medical school would probably cost too much, and you wouldn't be able to afford the tuition. You have already determined your failure by the words you allowed to come out of your mouth. Child of God, you began to talk yourself out of the blessing of accomplishing a goal you had set for yourself. You started speaking negative words against yourself and that which you were trying to accomplish. Those words counteracted the positive faith-filled words you had spoken before, those powerful words that had once come out of your mouth. Those bad confessions resulted in you still hoping and wishing you were a doctor --- saving peoples' lives the way you once dreamed you would.

    Child of God, this is not how God wants your life to turn out, no matter what your goals are. Just as He spoke all good things into existence, He left that same example for us to follow. Not for us to speak doubt and unbelief, but words that will bring success, health, happiness, peace, and prosperity into our lives. ***"...whatever a man sows, that and that only is what he will reap. For he who sows to his own flesh (lower nature, sensuality) will from the flesh reap decay and ruin and destruction; but he who sows to the Spirit will from the Spirit reap life eternal. (Galatians 6:6-8 AMP)***

God will not be made a fool of. If you sow negative, fear-based words in your heart, you will reap the harvest of those negative words spoken. Speaking negative words is an example of sowing to the flesh. As you speak God's words you sow to the Spirit.

Whatever you speak will come to pass, fleshly words or spiritual ones.

From God's perspective the words we speak are to be filled with so much faith, that they bring to us all the goodness and joy we desire for our lives.

If we take the time out to learn what God has to say on the subjects of our lives, and speak what God says, we'll never want for anything because, we'll have everything we've said.

Chapter Two
Watching Your Words

Set a guard, O Lord, before my mouth; keep a watch at the door of my lips.

Incline my heart not to submit or consent to any evil thing, or be occupied in the deeds of wickedness with men that work iniquity, and let me not eat of their dainties. (Psalm 141:3)

If any one thinks himself to be religious --- piously observant of the external duties of his faith --- and does not bridle his tongue, but deludes his own heart, this person's religious service is worthless (futile, barren) (James 1:26 AMP)

What James is saying here is that if a man is concerned about making himself look good and better than others by his religious acts, this man's religion is in vain. There is no power in a religion that will not enable a man to bridle his tongue. Are you constantly using your mouth in the wrong way, over and over again?

Our prayer to the Lord should be that He will help us with our mouths by setting a watch over them. Notice, I said we are praying. Prayer is what it takes to enable us to be disciplined enough to guard what we say. When you pray, the Holy Ghost who dwells on the inside of you, is there to help you with your infirmities. You are not to practice wicked works with men and eat their dainties, or in other words, talk the way they talk. As a Christian, you should not be looking for a way to sin, but for a way out of sin.

God judges a man by his heart. Every time you open your mouth to speak, your tongue is recording what you say on your heart. God reads what is written on your heart and brings only His Word to pass, if they are spoken in faith. God is not obligated to bring to pass the words of the devil. But, God will allow those words to come to pass in your life, if you so choose. By operating in fear and not in faith, you make the choice between blessings and curses.

My heart is inditing a good matter: I speak of the things which I have made touching the king: my tongue is the pen of a ready writer. (Psalm 45:1)

Your tongue is the pen that writes the words you speak on your heart. Look at it this way--- a pen has to have ink in order for you to write with it. Where does your ink come from? The ink is the Word of God. Indelibly written in my heart is the Word of God, which I have spoken regarding the circumstances and situations in my life. I speak only those things that please Jesus who is Lord over my life. He only speaks those things God spoke. You should only speak what Jesus spoke. Do so Child of God, and everything you say <u>shall</u> come to pass.

Even so the tongue is a little member, and boasteth great things. Behold, how great a matter a little fire kindleth!

And the tongue is a fire, a world of iniquity: so is the tongue among our members, that it defileth the whole body, and setteth on fire the course of nature; and it is set on fire of hell.

For every kind of beasts, and of birds, and of serpents, and of things in the sea, is tamed, and hath been tamed of mankind:

But the tongue can no man tame; it is an unruly evil, full of deadly poison.
Therewith bless we God, even the Father; and therewith curse we men, which are made after the similitude of God.

Out of the same mouth proceedeth blessing and cursing. My brethren, these things ought not so to be. (James 3:5-10)

In this chapter, James is revealing how effective the little thing in your mouth, called the tongue can be. Your tongue has the ability to set your whole body aflame. The words you speak can very well be dangerous, or they can provide comfort. They can either heal, kill or destroy the body. And, according to ***Proverbs 18:21, "Death and life are in the power of the tongue; and they that love it shall eat the fruit thereof."***

The only way your tongue can be tamed is through the Word of God. Once you receive Jesus Christ (The Anointed One and His Anointing), as your Lord and Savior, all of the power you need to overcome any circumstance or situation in your life is on the inside of you. Therefore, you have the ability to tame your tongue by way of the power on the inside of you. The power on the inside of you is the burden-removing, yoke-destroying power of God, which is the anointing. The Holy Spirit has been sent to assist you in every area of your life.

But ye shall receive power, after that the Holy Ghost is come upon you: and ye shall be witnesses unto me both in Jerusalem, and in all Judaea, and in Samaria, and unto the uttermost part of the earth. (Acts 1:8)

But the Comforter, which is the Holy Ghost, whom the Father will send in my name, he shall teach you all things, and bring all things to your remembrance, whatsoever I have said unto you. (John 14:26)

There is a system in which God wants us to operate, and it is called the Kingdom of God. The Kingdom of God is God's way of doing what He does. He has given us 66 books on how we are to conduct our lives. It is up to you to decide whether or not you will follow His instructions. But I will tell you this, it's not a debate, it's a decision. Do you know that if you choose not to live for Jesus, you will by default have chosen to live for Satan? Whether you choose consciously or not, the decision will be made.

***Deuteronomy 30:19** says, "I call heaven and earth to record this day against you, that I have set before you life and death, blessings and curses: therefore choose life, that both thou and thy seed may live..."*

Do you fully understand what this scripture is saying? The choices you make in life will even affect your seed. What will you choose? Will it be life or death? If you choose life, you have chosen to live the eternal life in heaven. If you choose death, which means everlasting destruction according to

2 Thessalonians 1:9, you will be eternally separated from God into the pit of hell. The Word of God says a good man leaves an inheritance to his children, and to their children. ***(Proverbs 13:22)*** Will your inheritance to your children and grandchildren be heaven, or hell?

If you choose death (which means everlasting destruction according to

2 Thessalonians 1:9), you will be separated from God into the pit of hell, eternally. My God! Will your decision have your children spend eternity in heaven or hell? The Word of God says a good man leaves an inheritance to his children, and to their children. (***Proverbs 13:22***) Will your inheritance to your children and their children be heaven, or hell?

CHAPTER THREE
RELATIONSHIPS THAT ARE AFFECTED BY THE WORDS WE SPEAK

We are involved in many different relationships on a daily basis. Regardless of the nature of the relationship --- marriage, parent and child, employer and employee --- they are Satan's primary targets. If Satan can break up a relationship of any kind, he can ultimately affect the church. Well, how can he do that? If he breaks up these relationships, he places each one in a position of offense, strife, envy or jealousy and ultimately affects your ability to clearly hear from God. You see, the church is made up of people who form relationships with one another. This is how he tries to attack the church --- through our relationships with one another.

Satan's objective is to cause confusion in the Body of Christ, and come between the relationship of two or more people. The marital relationship is a prime target for strife. Since the family is God's first line of defense, Satan has a field day with husbands and wives. We established earlier that the Kingdom of God is His way of doing what He does. But if you're not born again, you will not understand God's way of doing what He does. Better yet, you cannot understand how God wants you to operate in this world. We live in this world, but we do not operate our lives like those in the world operate their lives. God has set us apart from the world through His Word. *(John 17:14-17)*

Say for example, your husband is presently unemployed and therefore can't provide for you the way either of you would like. But every time you come home, he's sitting on the couch watching television instead of job hunting. How should you respond? Not by speaking cruel and ungodly words into his life, that's for sure. What is inside of your heart will eventually come out. The Bible says that out of the abundance of the heart the mouth speaks. *(Matthew 12:34)* So, let's just say the goodness of God is not being manifested in you today. You come home and he's in the same position you left him in when you went to work earlier that morning. The ultimate test is how you will respond. You want to deposit good, positive, faith-filled words that sound something like this: "Honey, how was job hunting today? Well, I have confidence that you will soon find a good, stable job with good pay. I love you, and I know you're doing everything you can to find a job to support us. I'll keep praying for you." Now, if he's not doing that, you're speaking it into existence, and God will honor your request. I know you're probably thinking that sounds corny, but in situations in my life when I responded in that manner, the burden was removed and the yoke was destroyed. Because in God's Word He says, ***"a soft answer curbs wrath, but the mouth of a fool will speak foolishness. (Proverbs 15:1-2)***

Let's suppose your spouse has a weight problem. If you're a person with a weight problem, you don't want someone constantly reminding you of this. To berate a person because of their size is both ungodly and unfair. To respond in any way other than a compassionate way may cause them to become offended. The word "offended" broken into two words would be 'off, ended' --- which means one has gotten <u>off</u> the Word and <u>ended</u> the process of speaking or receiving faith-filled words. When you speak negative words, you cancel out the positive words written on your heart. Words cut deeply into the heart. Problems in a marriage occur when couples are not communicating effectively, or when they are not choosing encouraging, uplifting words. When couples don't have the answers to their marital problems, they will seek a divorce instead of godly counsel. Even if the couple truly loves one another, often they can't figure out how to solve their problems. Some people will even make things worse than they really are by convincing themselves that their marriage is failing. They will begin to speak against their marriage by sowing bad seeds into their hearts regarding their situation. "It will never work. I might as well divorce him. He doesn't take care of me like he should anyway. He doesn't treat me like I feel I should be treated." Couples lash out at each other with words when they should be using words to strengthen their marriage and encourage each other.

What happened to the vows people make to each other? Those vows are for the better. We won't make the bad confession by saying "and worse" because we want to speak positive things about our marriages. The words we speak sometimes lead to our own worse nightmares.

Are you getting the picture of how your words can affect another person's life? Communication is one of the key ingredients in a marriage. If you are not communicating in a positive manner, you are communicating in a negative manner. Some of us will not even admit that we don't know enough about how to communicate with one another. If you are at this point in your marriage, I suggest you seek godly counseling.

BLESSED --- HAPPY, fortunate, prosperous and enviable --- is the man who walks and lives not in the counsel of the ungodly [following their advice, their plans and purposes] nor stands [submissive and inactive] in the path where sinners walk, nor sits down [to relax and rest] where the scornful [and the mockers] gather. (Psalm 1:1 AMP)

Not all people have your best interests at heart. Just because a person is saved, doesn't mean God has given them the answer for your particular situation. You should pray and ask the Father whom you should consult for counseling. If you are not sure, always seek advice from those who have been placed in authority at your local church. Many situations can easily be resolved without any outside interference. God loves you, and He wants you to be healed in every area of your life. God is concerned about everything you're involved in. The answers are just waiting on the inside of you.

HE CALLED ME OUT OF MY NAME

Words can hurt, and cause a person to feel discriminated against. In a situation where people can possibly become offended based on how you address them, remember to think before you speak. Using slang and vulgar terms to describe someone is not only disrespectful, it's not Christ-like. Calling a person "out of their name" as the saying goes, is not something people of God should get involved in. If this happens to you, if you find yourself the victim of racially motivated or gender-based insults, there's only one thing to do. Respond in a kind manner, and pray for the person who has touched you with his or her mouth. Don't repay evil with evil. Don't ever involve yourself in a conversation that starts with name-calling and racial slurs, not even jokingly. God has made the awesome power of words available to us for blessings and not to misuse them, or abuse others with them.

Let it never be said of those of you who count yourselves as children of the King, that this sinful act originated with you. We are all one in Christ. The Word of God says there is no male nor female, no slave nor free in the eyes of God. He sees only one thing when it comes to differentiating us, and that is whether we're saved or unsaved. Shouldn't you follow in your Father's footsteps and look at people the same way?

CAN'T WE ALL JUST GET ALONG?

Why are people called out of their names anyway? People are usually angry and hurt when they speak unkindly to one another. See Child of God, hurt people hurt others, offended people offend others, oppressed people oppress others and abusive people will abuse other people. It's a vicious cycle and we must put an end to it.

You've probably experienced some type of racial discrimination if you're living in this world today. But how you respond the next time when an offender tries to offend you with a racial comment is based on your seeing people the way God sees them. Yes, a person might call you out of your name, but you must get to a point where it doesn't offend you. You should know who and whose you are by now, and that is a Child of God. You are a gift from God, and every good and perfect gift comes from the Father above. *(James 1:17)*

Chapter Four
Gossiping is a Kingdom Issue

I believe with all my heart that people don't really understand how tremendously destructive gossip can be to themselves and others. Gossiping is a kingdom issue that will affect the anointing on your life. The Word of God has a lot to say about gossips, backbiters, and people who slander others. Tragically, some of us have not searched the scriptures to even know that this subject is dealt with in the Bible. Let's look at what God has to say about this issue. The gospel of Jesus Christ is this:

The gospel is the good news about *"**How God anointed Jesus of Nazareth with the Holy Ghost and with power: who went about doing good, and healing all that were oppressed of the devil; for God was with Him." (Acts 10:38)***

God placed an anointing on Jesus for Him to do good to all who needed to be healed and delivered from the devil. The Apostle Paul went to the church of the people in Corinth many times in regards to their sin. He appealed to them to repent, but the people of Corinth did whatever they wanted to do. In *2 Corinthians 12:20 (AMP)* Paul appeals again to the people regarding their sin. *"For I am fearful that somehow or other I may come and find you not as I desire to find you, and that you may find me too. Not as you want to find me --- that perhaps there may be factions, (quarreling, jealousy, temper, wrath, intrigues, rivalry, divided loyalties) selfishness, whispering, gossip, arrogance (self-assertion), and disorder among you."*

Paul was concerned that when he returned, the people were still going to be in sin. They had not listened to a word this man of God had to say. They couldn't care less about what would happen to them if they continued in their sin. They enjoyed sowing to the flesh. It didn't matter who was hurt in the process, the only thing that mattered was pleasing themselves.

Paul was not an ordinary man. He was an apostle sent by the Holy Spirit to minister to the people. Paul was a representative of God. In other words, he was symbolic of your pastor telling you to get out of sin and give your life to Jesus. When you disobey God, your pastor and all those in authority over you, you are in rebellion. What do you think will happen to you? Now if you said, "Oh nothing," or "maybe I won't prosper like I should," or something to that effect, you are sadly mistaken. Let's take a look at what the book of Romans has to say about what could happen to you. In the Amplified Bible version of ***Romans 1:28-32,*** it says, ***"And so, since they did not see fit to acknowledge God or approve of Him or consider worth the knowing, God gave them over to a base (worthless) and condemned mind to do things not proper or decent but loathsome. Until they were filled (permeated and saturated) with every kind of unrighteousness, iniquity, grasping and covetous greed and malice. (They were) full of envy and jealousy, murder, strife, deceit and treachery, ill will and cruel ways. (They were secret backbiters and gossipers, slanderers, hateful to and hating God, full of insolence, arrogance and boasting; inventors of new forms of evil, disobedient and undutiful to parents. (They were) without understanding, conscienceless and faithless, heartless and loveless and***

merciless. Though they are fully aware of God's righteous decree that those who do such things deserve to die (be separated from God) they not only do themselves, but approve and applaud others who practice them."

God is concerned about His people and how they are conducting themselves. If you choose to act foolishly, by not obeying the laws established for us in the Word of God, you have chosen to serve Satan. That might seem a little harsh, but it's true. Just writing this has made me repent and judge myself in some areas. I have to continue to rid my own heart of junk, do a clean sweep every now and then. I never want to be separated from the presence of God. Can you imagine how dark that place is? You are on your way to hell if you continue to operate like those folks in the previous scripture. You cannot keep professing to be a Christian while acting like a heathen. My pastor is constantly keeping me in line with the Word of God, and he doesn't cut corners. I can strongly say that if he did cut corners and compromise the Word, I would not be in the blessed position I'm in today. A parent corrects his children in love.

The Word talks about a person who loves strife, is quarrelsome, loves transgression and involves himself in guilt. ***"He who raises high his gateway and is boastful and arrogant invites destruction." (Proverbs 17:19 AMP)*** In other words, a person who loves strife and argues with others and loves sin, also invites himself into guilt and condemnation. If a man opens himself up to entertain boastfulness and is arrogant, he invites his own destruction.

You are slowly killing yourself when you get involved in gossip, backbiting, strife, envy and jealousy. This affects your entire body. Think about it, when you're in strife with someone or jealous of them, you can't eat or sleep. You keep worrying about what that person is doing, saying or might even be accomplishing. You may even have headaches from the worry. You find yourself always talking about that person. You even make yourself look and sound stupid from the type of comments you make regarding this individual.

Change how you see yourself and those you gossip about. Start focusing in on what is best for you in your walk with Christ. The Word of God has this to say: ***"Moreover, as they go about from house to house, they learn to be idlers, and not only idlers, but gossips and busybodies, saying what they should not say and talking of things they should not mention." (1 Timothy 5:13 AMP) "A perverse man sows strife, and a whisperer separates close friends." (Proverbs 16:28 AMP)***

We can look at these scriptures and find that the Bible knows a lot about how we are living. When you read the two previous scriptures, it seems as if the writer knew who you were personally. You have a serious gossiping and busybody problem if you saw yourself in these scriptures, and you need to quickly repent. Understand that repentance is not just saying you're sorry for being a gossip and a busybody. When you say you're sorry, you might just be sorry that you were caught. Repentance is a change of heart and mind with the decision to turn away from sin.

I feel like the Apostle Paul right about now. Are you reading and understanding the points I'm making in this book? If you want to change, then you should begin praying for the person with whom you're in strife. While in the presence of God, He will begin to restore your relationship. In the process, you'll be edified by the Word and prayer.

WHY DO WE GOSSIP?

How does it make you feel when someone is gossiping about you? Do you lash out, or do you stand still until those who hear the lie will come to the knowledge of the truth? The Word of God talks about praying for those who despitelfully use you. *(Luke 6:28)* I know that it's hard to do sometimes, because people will get on your last nerve. But, the effectual, fervent prayer of a righteous man will avail much. Your prayer will bring the truth on the scene because you are righteous. Here is how the Amplified Bible puts it: ***Confess to one another therefore your faults, (your slips, your false steps, your offense, your sins) and***

pray (also) for one another, that you may be healed and restored (to a spiritual tone of mind and heart. The earnest (heartfelt, continued) prayer of a righteous man makes tremendous power available (that is dynamic in its working). (James 5:16 AMP) Your prayer will have enough power to remove your burden and destroy your yoke. The burden and yoke in your life right now could be someone who is gossiping about you. When you pray for them, the Lord will turn their heart to pray for you. Therefore, you are praying one for another.

Now, in that scripture it talks about telling each other your faults. You'd better make sure you tell someone you can trust, and not someone who will tell the whole world your faults. Usually when a person is talking about you, someone is probably talking about them. Remember, they may have one finger pointing at you, but four are pointing back at them. There is a root to all the evil we involve ourselves in. A liar is drawn to other liars. You know the saying, "misery loves company." Gossips are drawn to those who love to gossip. The saga could go on and on. If we have not dealt with the deep hurts within us, we will begin to hurt and find fault in others.

First of all, a person who gossips needs to recognize that they have too much work to do in their own lives to be concerned about others. People gossip because they really don't want to deal with their own problems. How can you tell a gossip? They're the ones who call every day and have nothing to say. Usually, they will begin to make things up. They'll ask you on the sly if you've heard from the person they plan to talk about. They never discuss their situations, they always want to talk about others. Or, here's a real good one --- "we need to pray for her." They will talk about the situation as if they're concerned about what the individual is going through.

People, we're going to have to start taking a closer look at how we're conducting ourselves. This is not just for our benefit, but for the benefit of those with whom we come into contact.

Chapter Five
The Mouth Is An Unruly Thing

O generation of vipers, how can ye, being evil speak good things? For out of the abundance of the heart, the mouth speaketh.

Whatever is in your heart will come out of your mouth. Jesus called a generation that spoke evil things, vipers. A viper is a snake, and a snake cannot be trusted. How would you like to be called a snake by Jesus? If you want to be spoken of in a positive way, then it is time to obey the Word of God where your mouth is concerned. God continues to command us on how we should use our mouths.

But now put away and rid yourselves (completely) of all these things: anger, rage, bad feelings toward others, curses and slander, and foulmouthed abuse, and shameful utterances from your lips! Do not lie to one another, for you have stripped off the old (unregenerated) self with its

evil practices, and have clothed yourselves with the new (spiritual self), which is ever in the process of being renewed and remolded into the image (the likeness) of Him who created it. (Colossians 3:8-10 AMP)

What's being said in this scripture, is that this way of talking should have been put away when you got born again. You should renew your mind daily with the Word of God. The Lord says to put on the whole armor of God, which is the Word of God. When you put on the Word, you are putting on the power of God. You learned earlier in another chapter that you are created in the image of God and in His likeness. God wants to mold you into His image. There are scriptures in which God specifically lets you know how your mouth is to be used. They also explain what happens when you do not obey His commands. When you read the next few scriptures, I want you to imagine God sitting at the table with you while you're studying. During your study time, He begins to deal with you regarding your mouth.

You give your mouth to evil, and your tongue frames deceit. You sit and speak against your brother, you slander your own mother's son. (Psalm 50:19-20)

For there is nothing trustworthy or steadfast or truthful in their talk, their heart is destruction (or a destructive chasm, a yawning gulf) their throat is an open sepulcher, they flatter and make smooth with their tongue. Hold them guilty, O God; let them fall by their own design and counsels; cast them out because of the multitude of their transgressions, for they have rebelled against you. (Psalm 5:9 AMP)

Let no foul or polluting language, nor evil word nor unwholesome or worthless talk (ever) come out of your mouth, but only such (speech) as is good and beneficial to the spiritual progress of others, as is fitting to the need and the occasion, that it may be a blessing and give grace (God's favor) to those who hear it. (Ephesians 4:29 AMP)

The mouth of the uncompromisingly righteous utters wisdom, and his tongue speaks with justice. The law of his God is in his heart, none of his steps shall slide. (Psalm 37:30-31 AMP)

This is the response you should give the Lord after you have repented for the deceitfulness of your talk:

I said I will take heed to my ways, that I sin not with my tongue; I will keep my mouth with a bridle, while the wicked is before me. (Psalm 39:1)

Set a guard, O Lord, before my mouth; keep watch at the door of my lips. Incline my heart not to submit or consent to any evil things, or to be occupied in deeds of wickedness with men who work iniquity; and let me not eat their dainties. (Psalm 141:3-4)

I will bless the Lord at all times; His praise shall continually be in my mouth. (Psalm 34:1)

This book of the law shall not depart out of thy mouth, but thou shalt meditate therein day and night, that thou mayest observe to do according to all that is written therein; for then thou shall make thy way prosperous, and then thou shalt have good success. (Joshua 1:8)

Thank Him for forgiving your sins.

Let the words of my mouth and the meditation of my heart be acceptable in thy sigh, O Lord, my strength, and my redeemer. (Psalm 19:14)

Chapter Six
Where Do I Go From Here?

Child of God, I'm going to tell you something right now that I don't ever want you to forget. GOD REALLY LOVES YOU! Once He has forgiven you of your sins, He remembers them no more. We are the only ones who keep reminding Him of what we did yesterday. We're going to have to stop feeling sorry for ourselves. Why are we always feeling that we're unworthy? I truly believe that if we continue to remind ourselves of that sin we used to be in, it's because we really don't believe Jesus cleansed us of our sins. How can you say God loves you, and that He forgave you, and you can't even forgive yourself? First of all, you must forgive yourself for all the wrong you've done, and allow Jesus to fully wrap His loving arms around you.

Therefore, (there is) now no condemnation (no adjudging guilty or wrong) for those who are in Christ Jesus, who live (and) walk not after the dictates of the flesh, but after the dictates of the Spirit. (Romans 8:1 AMP)

One thing I know for sure, and that is that the foundation of God, which is the Word of God, will stand forever. Once you get born again, God seals your heart with Christ Jesus. He circumcises your heart with the seal of The Anointed One and His Anointing, Jesus. The circumcision of this seal is not physical. You were spiritually circumcised. The Lord knows who you are by the seal on your heart. God weighs and reads the heart of a man.

According to ***2 Timothy 2:19***, God commands you to depart from iniquity or sin, when you call upon Jesus. We learned in an earlier chapter that the anointing is what removes your burdens and destroys your yokes. If you don't have control over your tongue, then your tongue is yoked up and burdened down. Now call the anointing on the scene! "How do I get the anointing on the scene?" Child of God, it is within you. When you call on the name of the Lord Jesus Christ, you are calling the anointing to come up out of you and on you. You must believe that the anointing is on the scene right then. You might not see the manifestation yet, but that's where the believing *'it is already done'* comes in.

Nothing will break the seal the Lord has placed on the inside of your heart. I'm not speaking of the physical heart that pumps blood. I'm referring to the spiritual heart. The inner heart of a man is his spirit. On the inside of you, there is a great house that Christ lives within. But, just because Christ lives within you doesn't mean that everything is okay. If you're not developing your spirit man, then your spirit is probably weak. Therefore, when circumstances and situations arise, your flesh will override your spirit because it is stronger.

I want you to begin to cultivate your spirit man by getting in the Word of God. There are several steps you must take in order to begin the process of cultivation. The first step is to read the Word of God on a daily basis. Open it and read the scriptures. When you open the Bible, and read the scriptures pertaining to your situation, the Lord will cause you to understand what you're reading.

The second step you must take is to study the scriptures you're reading. ***Study to shew thyself approved unto God a workman that needeth not be ashamed, rightly*** *dividing the word of truth. (2 Timothy 2:15)* If you don't know where a certain scripture is concerning your situation, use a concordance. Your Bible is equipped with a concordance in the back of the book; but, you can also purchase a good concordance if the one in your Bible is limited. Remember, the Bible is our manual for living.

The next thing you must do is meditate on the scriptures you've found. Meditating gets the Word on the inside of your heart. ***But his delight is in the law (God's Word) of the Lord; and in His law doth he meditate day and night. (Psalm 1:2) But thou shall meditate in the word day and night that thou mayest observe to do all that is written therein; for then thou shalt make thy way prosperous, and then thou shalt have good success. (Joshua 1:8)*** Once you understand the Word of God, you can do all that is written within it.

Last, but certainly not least, you can begin to speak to your circumstances. When speaking to your circumstances, you must speak to the root of the problem. If the problem is depression, then speak to the root of that problem which is the spirit of depression. If the problem is disobedience, then speak to the root spirit of disobedience until it has no power over you, you're now in control. If you don't take care of the problem, the problem will certainly take care of you.

Leave no such room or foothold for the devil, give no opportunity to him. (Ephesians 4:27 AMP)

Dig up the weeds in your life by building a foundation on the Word of God. Get the Word of God before your eyes, in your ears, on your mouth and in your heart so that you may live.

I'm not telling you anything you don't already know. But take heart to what I've said in this book. What you've done to the least of them, you've done it unto Jesus. The source of real power is the Word of God coming out of your mouth. Words are spiritual vehicles that carry inside of them the power to bring what has been spoken to pass. Remember, the main objective of those who gossip is to hurt, destroy, kill, cause conflict, or stir up strife. The destination for words of edification is restoration, healing spiritually and physically, love, life and kindness.

You already have what it takes on the inside of you to succeed and overcome your mouth. Learn how to tap into the anointing for success and overcome! And remember, GREET ME WITH A HOLY KISS!

21 DAYS OF MOUTH ALTERING CHANGE
DAILY STUDY GUIDE

This study guide is meant to help you think through how the words that you speak about yourself and others in diverse situations and circumstances, has the power to transform every aspect of your relationships. Thoughts and questions addressed in the following pages will help you to examine your relationships, your life and take important steps to become the cool, calm and collected person God intended you to be.

Use this study guide because you have purposed in your mind that "change is good". You can work through it on your own for personal development, as a part of a small group/book club, or even during a weekend retreat. I'm sure you know a couple of folks who would benefit from this book and mouth altering study guide. When reading the book make sure you take notes, highlight important areas, while working your way through the corresponding study guide, for maximum benefit.

The most effective way to use this study guide is to go through it on your own, even if you're also going to discuss it in a group setting or on a retreat. Taking the time to read through the chapters in the book and think through how each it can affect your life will give the study depth and immediate personal execution.

Because most of the questions are personal, if you use this study guide in a group setting or on a retreat, remember that courtesy and mutual respect lay the foundation for a healthy group. A small group should be a safe place for all who participate. Some of what will be shared is highly sensitive in nature and some may be controversial, so respect the confidentiality of the person who is sharing. Don't let your conversation leave the small group or turn into gossip. What happens in the group stays in the group! A small group is not a place to force opinions on others. Sometimes we need to keep our thoughts to ourselves and learn to be a good listener. Folks just want to get things off their chest, respect that. Commit yourself to listening to one another, be sensitive to their perspectives,

Greet Me With A Holy Kiss

and show them the grace and mercy you would like to receive from others.

"My Tongue is the Pen of a Ready Writer"

Psalm 45:1

**ENTERING YOUR MOUTH
ALTERING JOURNEY**

DAILY STUDY GUIDE
DAY 1

> ***Matthew 12:37***, *"For by thy words thou shalt be justified, and by thy words thou shalt be condemned."*

1. What was your immediate reaction and response when you read the introduction of this book? Did you think of a situation where you may have experienced or been a contributor?

   _____
   _____
   _____
   _____
   _____
   _____
   _____
   _____
   _____
   _____
   _____

2. What were the first three words that came to mind that you say on a regular basis?_____

   _____

   _____

3. How do you feel about using these words now that you have read this book?_____

   _____

   _____

   _____

   _____

   _____

Joshua 1:8, "This book of the law shall not depart out of thy mouth; but thou shalt meditate therein day and night, that thou mayest observe to do according to all that is written therein: for then thou shalt make thy way prosperous, and then thou shalt have good success.

4. How do your thoughts about yourself line up with the words you use on a daily basis?_____

_____
_____
_____
_____
_____

5. Do you ever wish you could take back what you said? Yes or No? Write why you answered the way you did. Why did you want to take it back or not?__

_____
_____
_____
_____
_____
_____
_____
_____
_____

> ***Psalms 19:4**, "Let the words of my mouth, and the meditation of my heart, be acceptable in Thy sight, O LORD, my strength, and my redeemer."*

MY CONFESSION

O LORD, my journey into the world of changing what I say and how I speak may be a little challenging but I just trust You are with me. Help me to mediate in Your word day and night so that I may not say something I will regret. I want to be acceptable in Your sight. I need Your strength to get through this. I know I can do it. I believe what I just confessed in Jesus Name, Amen.

DAILY STUDY GUIDE
DAY 2

> *Genesis*....In the beginning God Said! Everything God said in the beginning was a positive statement which resulted in a positive action.
> Let's speak some positive things out of your mouth.

- ♥ My mouth is a weapon of power.
- ♥ My mouth will be used to encourage.
- ♥ My mouth will speak of the goodness of the Lord.
- ♥ My mouth will not speak words of hate.
- ♥ My mouth will not cause strife.
- ♥ My mouth will not cause confusion.
- ♥ My mouth will not foster discrimination.
- ♥ My mouth will not cause discord.
- ♥ My mouth will not be unkind.
- ♥ My mouth will not be abusive to others.
- ♥ My mouth shall speak wisdom.
- ♥ I am an awesome father.

- ♥ I am an awesome mother.
- ♥ My family is blessed.
- ♥ I am an amazing parent.
- ♥ My relationships are blessed.
- ♥ I am empowered.
- ♥ I am well able.
- ♥ I am quick to forgive.
- ♥ I am quick to believe the best of myself and others.
- ♥ I am kind.
- ♥ I am secure.
- ♥ I am beautiful.
- ♥ I am victorious.
- ♥ I am success.
- ♥ I am free.
- ♥ I am delivered.
- ♥ I am confident.
- ♥ I prosper with everything I put my hands to.
- ♥ I am excited about life.
- ♥ I am happy.
- ♥ My mouth is ready for change.

DAILY STUDY GUIDE
DAY 3

> ***Hebrews 11:1 AMP***, *"Now faith is the assurance, (the confirmation, the title deed) of things (we) hope for, being the proof of things (we) do not see, and the conviction of their reality (faith perceiving as real fact what is not revealed to the senses.)*

1. If faith is the substance and the manifestation of things hoped for, describe at least one thing you are believing God to become a tangible reality in your life._____

    _____
    _____
    _____
    _____
    _____
    _____

2. Name (7) things where you have used your faith and it has come to pass?_____

_____
_____
_____
_____
_____
_____
_____
_____
_____
_____

If you couldn't come up with (7) things, don't fret. This is an opportunity for you to believe God for something and watch Him bring it to pass.

DAILY STUDY GUIDE
DAY 4

Now some things may make you raise an eyebrow as you go through this study guide but your goal is to experience some mouth altering changes. Keep doing this, it's going to help you.

"Thus says the LORD of host: Consider your ways"

Haggai 1:7

1. Based upon the words you speak on a daily basis, are you speaking healing, wholeness, and breakthroughs?__
_____
_____
_____
_____

_____
_____
_____
_____
_____

2. Think for a moment about how you start your day? Is prayer apart of your day? Write a short prayer that you can say each morning that reflects how you are working on your mouth. Make a point to declare your prayer boldly each morning._____

_____
_____
_____
_____
_____
_____

MY CONFESSION

      O LORD, You have to help me with this mouth of mine. I have faith I can change. I declare healing over my life. I am whole and complete. I don't lack anything because You are my provider. I will continue to work on this. I will not be defeated. Consistency is the key to my breakthrough. I believe what I just confessed in Jesus Name, Amen…

"Keep thy heart with all diligence; for out of it flows the issues of life"

Proverbs 4:23

Greet Me With A Holy Kiss

DAILY STUDY GUIDE
DAY 5

> ***Psalms 141:1**, Set a guard, O Lord, before my mouth; keep a watch at the door of my lips.*

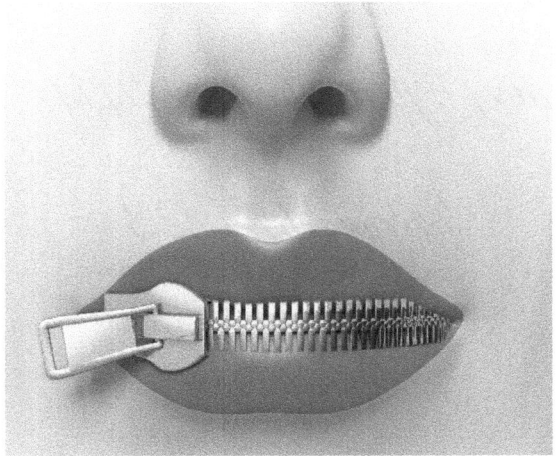

1. Have you ever sensed God was telling you to ZIP IT? Did you ZIP IT or did you just let it RIP?_____

   _____
   _____
   _____

2. Are you constantly using your mouth in the wrong way, over and over again?_____

    _____

    _____

    _____

    _____

3. What situations or areas in your life are you facing that immediately set you off and causes you to use your mouth in an unfavorable manner?_____

    _____

    _____

    _____

    _____

    _____

4. Do you believe that negative, degrading speech can stop God's promises? Describe how you feel._____

    _____

    _____

    _____

DAILY STUDY GUIDE
DAY 6

Psalm 45:1*, My heart is inditing a good matter: I speak of things which I have made touching the king: my tongue is the pen of a ready writer.*

1. Read Psalms 45:1 again. Write the definition of these words. Inditing, speak, ready._____
   _____
   _____
   _____

_____
_____
_____

2. Once you've changed the way you have been communicating, what transformation are you hoping for as a result of that change?_____

_____
_____
_____
_____

Words are creative power. When God created the worlds, He didn't just think them into being. He spoke what He was thinking into existence. Answer all which applies.

3. Write down some positive words about yourself._____

_____
_____
_____
_____
_____

4. Write down some positive words about your children.__
   _____
   _____
   _____
   _____

5. Write down some positive words about your spouse.__
   _____
   _____
   _____
   _____

6. Write down some positive words about your mother-in-law._____
   _____
   _____
   _____

"Let the Redeemed of the Lord Say So" Psalms 107:2

DAILY STUDY GUIDE
DAY 7

> ***James 3:5-10***, *Out of the same mouth proceedeth blessings and cursing. My brethren, these things ought not to be so.*

1. Describe an instance when you spoke blessings over your life or someone else._____
   _____
   _____
   _____

2. The blessings you spoke, did they come to pass?_____
   _____
   _____
   _____

3. Describe a situation that will cause you to curse?_____
   _____
   _____
   _____
   _____

4. How did you feel after you cursed the wall paper off the wall?_____
   _____
   _____
   _____

5. Let's look at a cursing in another aspect. Describe a time where you spoke a curse on someone? Example: I hope you go to hell with YO UGLY SELF. _____
   _____
   _____
   _____
   _____
   _____

"Lord this ought NOT to be So"

DAILY STUDY GUIDE
DAY 8

> ***John 17:14-17***, *God has set us apart from the world through His Word. We are sanctified through the truth of His Word.*

1. Describe an issue in your life that you've struggled with for a long time. After reading this book, how do you view that situation now?_____

   _____
   _____
   _____
   _____
   _____

2. To break the stronghold that has taken place in your heart, what is the immediate action you plan to take?___

   _____
   _____
   _____
   _____

3. You mouth has to get into agreement with God. It is time to let go and be free. Affirm it here by writing a confession of what you are believing God to do through you._____

_____
_____
_____
_____
_____
_____
_____
_____

4. How are you feeling about the study guide so far? Is it helping you to see things a little more clearly?_____

_____
_____
_____
_____
_____

"I can see clearly now the Dark Cloud is Gone. I can see all Obstacle's in my Way"

DAILY STUDY GUIDE
DAY 9

> ***Matthew 12:34**, Out of the abundance of the heart the mouth speaks.*

If you confess with your mouth, "Jesus is Lord," and believe in your heart that God raised him from the dead, you will be saved. For it is with your heart that you believe and are justified, and it is with your mouth that you confess and are saved. As the Scripture says, "Anyone who trust in Him will never be put to shame." The same Lord is Lord of all and richly blesses all who call on Him for, "Everyone who calls on the name of the Lord will be saved."

1. Have you called upon the name of the Lord Jesus to help you with your mouth transformation?_____

    _____
    _____
    _____
    _____

2. Have you believed with your heart and confessed with your mouth that Jesus is your Lord?_____

    _____
    _____
    _____

3. Answering 1 and 2 brings us to this point. You have all the power on the inside of you to make the necessary changes to be a better you. Are you going to trust God to help you? If so, write down your steps to make this happen. Example: I will do this and I will not to that; as a result, I will change._____

    _____
    _____
    _____

_____
_____
_____
_____
_____
_____

MY CONFESSION

O LORD, You said You would never leave me, You said you would never forsake me. I believe You can make me free from what I am presently going through right now. Create in me a clean heart, a clean mouth, and a clean mind. I live to do Your will not mine. I believe what I just confessed in Jesus Name, Amen.

DAILY STUDY GUIDE
DAY 10

> ***Proverbs 23:7***, *For as he thinketh in his heart, so is he: Eat and drink, saith he to thee; but his heart is not with thee.*

Think new thoughts and a new way of living. No matter where you are in life right now, God has much more in store for you in your relationships, on your job, in your marriage, with your children. But let me tell you, you have to allow God to be the center of everything you do. He is ready to take you to another level. With new levels there will be new devils. You can handle it with God on your side. The enemy will not be able to overrule you with God ordering and directing your steps. God wants to take you to new levels in every area of your life. He wants to give you more wisdom so you can make godly decisions and not make bad decisions. Don't get stuck in the old way of doing things. Same old same old! Your best days are looking you right in the face.

Begin today to think the way God thinks. See yourself like God sees you. You may be asking yourself right now who in the world can think like God? Simple, God's mindset is His Word.

1. Describe your thoughts and feelings after reading today's study guide._____
_____
_____
_____
_____
_____
_____
_____
_____

DAILY STUDY GUIDE
DAY 11

> ***Hebrews 10:35**, Do not cast away your confidence for it will be richly rewarded.*

Dear Heavenly Father, I commit my thoughts to You today. I purpose in my heart to stay focused on You and the good plan You have for my life today in all my situations. Holy Spirit please remind me of God's Word so I can fill my heart and my mouth with His promises. Help me to not throw away my confidence in the midst of situations that may cause me to doubt. I have the victory over every area of my life.

1. Write the definition of confidence._____
   _____
   _____
   _____
   _____

2. Describe confidence in your own words._____
   _____
   _____
   _____
   _____
   _____

3. Write down as many synonyms as you can think of._____
   _____
   _____
   _____
   _____

4. Now write down as many words opposite of confidence. Unconfident...._____
   _____
   _____
   _____
   _____
   _____
   _____

5. Which will you walk in confidence or unconfident?_____
   _____
   _____
   _____

DAILY STUDY GUIDE
DAY 12

"I Need to Let Go of the Past"

Learning to let go maybe one the hardest things to do in life. But letting go is how you overcome situations and circumstances. Letting go of the hurts, disappointments, and who did what to you. Choosing to forgive those that have wronged you. Choosing to forgive yourself for the wrong you've done to others. Don't let yesterday's regrets destroy your hopes of restoration for tomorrow. No matter what happened in the past you can let it go. God is a God of restoration, and He will restore what the enemy thought he stole from you. He thought he stole your peace, joy, love, mind, your willingness to do good. Nope, he is a liar. Devil you lose! Accept God's grace and mercy today. I call these the "Do Over Twins". Grace and Mercy have the power and ability to do it all over again. Glory to God!

1. Write down something you have had a hard time letting go of._____

   _____
   _____
   _____
   _____
   _____
   _____

2. Now this is what I want you to do with that paper from #1. Take that piece of paper and burn it! Don't start a fire somewhere, burn it in a safe place. I don't want nobody to burn down the house today.

Can I pause right here and say how much I love you? I am right here with you. I know where you are because I have been there. Critical points in my life have been burned. I know you can overcome because I have. If I can do it, I have great confidence you can too.

DAILY STUDY GUIDE
DAY 13

> ***Joshua 1:8**, This book of the law shall not depart out of thy mouth; but thou shalt meditate therein day and night, that thou mayest observe to do according to all that is written therein: for then thou shalt make thy way prosperous, and then thou shalt have good success.*

Confessions is good for the spirit, soul and body. Meditate today on God's Word. Grab your bible, pen and writing tablet. Read these scriptures today and write down what you hear God is saying to you.

1. ***John 17:14-17*** – God has set us apart from the world through His Word.
2. ***Proverbs 15:1-2*** – A soft answer turns away wrath, but the mouth of a fool will speak foolishness.
3. ***Psalms 19:4*** – Let the words of my mouth, and the mediation of my heart, be acceptable in thy sight, O LORD, my strength, and my redeemer.
4. ***Genesis 1:26*** – God said, Let Us (Father, Son and Holy Spirit) make mankind in Our image, after Our likeness; and let them have complete authority over the fish of the sea, the birds of the air, the (tame) beasts, and over all the earth, and over everything that creeps upon the earth. Today you have authority over creeps.
5. ***Mark 11:24*** – The world says, "seeing is believing," but the Word says "believe and you will see."

6. ***Galatians 6:6-8*** – Whatever a man sows, that and that only is what he will reap.
7. ***Proverbs 18:21*** – Death and life are in the power of the tongue; and they that love it shall eat the fruit thereof.
8. ***Hebrews 10:35*** – Do not cast away your confidence for it will be richly rewarded.
9. ***Joel 2:25-26*** – I will restore the years that the locust has eaten and I will bring you out with plenty and you shall be satisfied.
10. ***Deuteronomy 30:19*** – I call heaven and earth to record this day against you, that I have set before you life and death, blessing and curses: therefore choose life, that both thou and thy seed may live.

DAILY STUDY GUIDE
DAY 14

"Can I Live A Life Of Contentment?"

1. Write the definition of content._____

   _____
   _____
   _____
   _____

2. Write the definition of contentment._____

   _____
   _____
   _____
   _____

3. Write the definition of frustrated._____

   _____
   _____
   _____
   _____

4. On a scale of 1 to 10, with 1 being frustrated and discontent and 10 being content, how would you grade yourself? Describe where you are currently.___

_____
_____
_____
_____
_____
_____

5. What do you believe God is trying to work in your life as you work through this study guide?_____

_____
_____
_____
_____
_____
_____
_____

6. Describe a situation where you feel you had to exercise being content. _____
_____
_____
_____
_____
_____
_____

DAILY STUDY GUIDE
DAY 15

"Learn To Love Yourself"

Today let's talk about learning to love yourself. You have to learn to be secure in who you are. How do you do that? Become secure in who you are in Christ Jesus.

1. Do you sometimes feel you are pressured to climb the ladder of success by stepping on other folks to get there? Has that pressure succeeded at times?___
_____

_____
_____
_____
_____
_____

2. What gifts and talents do you believe God has given you? What basically gets you stirred up every day?_
_____
_____
_____
_____
_____
_____
_____

3. Are you working on what God has called you to do or are you working on what God has called someone else to do?_____
_____
_____
_____

Not being in the will of God for your life and living out

someone else's dream can cause you to think and speak differently at times. Coveting another person's gift can get frustrating at times because you should be doing what God has called you to do. When you are in the will of God for your life it causes you to think and speak positively.

4. Tell me about your vision and dreams that God has given you._____

_____

_____

_____

_____

_____

_____

_____

5. What is your plan to start doing what God has called you to do? It may be a better Mom or Dad. Be a better employee. Write a book. Be a faithful servant in ministry. Write it down and make it plain, then run with it. *Habakkuk 2:3*_____

Greet Me With A Holy Kiss

_____
_____
_____
_____
_____
_____
_____
_____
_____
_____
_____

"Be Comfortable With You!"

DAILY STUDY GUIDE
DAY 16

"Let The Redeemed of the Lord Say So"

Speak these positive things over your life today.

- ♥ When preparation meets opportunity, I will have success.
- ♥ The right opportunities are on my path.
- ♥ The right people that can help push me to greatness is seeking me out.
- ♥ My steps are ordered of the Lord because I am traveling down the right road.
- ♥ I am comfortable in who I am.
- ♥ I will become all that God has created me to be.
- ♥ I always finish what I start.
- ♥ My visions, dreams and legacy will live on to inspire generations to come.

♥ I am the redeemed of the Lord, and I say so today!

DAILY STUDY GUIDE
DAY 17

> ***James 1:7-8***, *Let not that man think that he shall receive anything from the Lord. A double minded man is unstable in all his ways.*

1. What are you doing right now? Are you trying to figure out what to do? _____
   _____
   _____
   _____
   _____
   _____

2. Do you spend more time trying to figure out was it you, God or the devil? God is not going to tell you anything and not back it up with His Word. Write down the struggle. What's confusing you?
   _____

3. Write down what you are going to do about it?_____

_____

_____

_____

DAILY STUDY GUIDE

DAY 18

> ***Ephesians 4:29***, *Let no foul or polluting language come out of your mouth.*

1. How often do you find yourself complaining about a situation?_____

_____

_____

_____

Newsflash – complaining is not based on your circumstances and situations; it's based on your attitude. The attitude of the heart. A heart full of gratitude leaves no room for complaining.

2. Write down the things you are grateful for._____

_____

_____

_____

_____

3. Take a few minutes right now and thank God for giving you a life. Take 3 deep breaths now.
4. Write down how you feel after completing question three._____

_____

_____

_____

_____

_____

MY CONFESSION

Dear Heavenly Father, I am so grateful for all you have done for me. I thankful for Your love, joy, and peace. I'm thankful for Your faithfulness even when I am not. I am thankful for the situations you have brought me through and are bringing me through. May the words of my mouth and the meditations of my heart be acceptable in Your sight all the days of my life.

DAILY STUDY GUIDE
DAY 19

> ***Philippians 3:13-14**, This one thing I do, forgetting what lies behind, I press towards the mark.....*

1. How do you plan to be aggressive about moving forward and pressing on?_____
   _____
   _____

_____
_____
_____
_____

2. How will you implement your mouth in this process?
_____
_____
_____
_____
_____
_____

3. Set some boundaries when you feel like you may be headed back to old habits?_____
_____
_____
_____
_____
_____
_____
_____

4. Write down some triggers so you can be aware when things start to go downhill for you._____

_____
_____
_____
_____
_____

"Press On"

DAILY STUDY GUIDE

DAY 20

"Let Not Your Heart Be Troubled: Ye Believe In God, Believe Also In Me" John 14:1

Today I want to focus on trusting God's timing. His timing is not your time. His ways are not your ways.

1. Write down some ways you are going to relax while waiting on God to manifest His promises._____

   _____
   _____
   _____
   _____
   _____
   _____

2. Do you trust God enough to believe your set time is coming?_____

   _____
   _____

_____
_____
_____
_____

3. Think of a situation where you did not trust God to wait until He came through. What do you think the outcome would have been had you waited? Be honest._____
_____
_____
_____
_____

DAILY STUDY GUIDE
DAY 21

"Expect God to Move Suddenly in your Life!"

I want to leave you with this powerful statement of encouragement that you can hang on to for the rest of your life. May God cause you to never forget it. It is expecting the Lord thy God to move suddenly in your life forever!

There may have been times in your life where you felt nothing was going to change. This is the way it has been, this is how I have been and nothing can change that. And you go and just go on, day to day existing in the life you've chosen to live in. But God! But God who is the God of the 'and suddenly' will turn things around for you. God heard your prayers and your confessions. He will remember them and you have to believe this. There is an end to your situation but you have to do your part too. Then suddenly He will move in your life and deliver you in a way that will make you say WOW, I'm like they that dream. ***Psalms 126:1***

Your hopelessness will turn into hope. Your mouth will bless and not curse. Your mind will be renewed to a new way of thinking. You are going to have to be patient and let patience have her perfect work in you. Waiting releases the anointing to get the job done. Waiting releases power, ability and might. Waiting brings life to a dead situation. How does it do that? Waiting allows you to not react suddenly. It allows you to see clearly. How long should I wait? As long as it takes. A great man of God told me a long time ago "If you are willing to wait forever, you won't be waiting long."

1. Are you willing to wait forever and experience the move of God in your life?_____
_____
_____
_____
_____

This concludes our study guide. Write me and let me know how this book has changed your life.

REDEDICATION OF YOUR MOUTH

Dear Heavenly Father,

I repent for using my mouth in all the wrong ways. I rededicate my mouth to You today. I set a watch over my mouth and lips so I can only speak those things which are true, honest, just, pure, lovely and of a good report. (Philippians 4:8) I make this commitment to You with all my heart to never again speak a bad report, degrade, or make a negative confession about a brother or sister in Christ, the Anointed One. I will only speak the best of someone. I make a decision to stop speaking negative confessions over my own life. I will begin to speak the Word of God only over my circumstances, saying the Word of God and seeing it come to pass immediately. I make the decision to be a doer of the Word, and not just a hearer only.

Thank You Lord for forgiving me and releasing me of my sins. In the name of Jesus, I pray. Amen.

Signature_____
Date_____

Sign here to remind yourself that you have made this commitment to God.

Deneen Whatley

ENTERING INTO A NEW LIFE

There are a few steps you must be made aware of before entering into your new life. When you complete these three steps by confessing and praying them, you become born again.

First of all, YOU MUST ADMIT THAT YOU ARE A SINNER. According to **Psalm 51:5, "I was shapen in iniquity, and in sin did my mother conceive me."** All you needed to have done to become a sinner was to be born into this world. When Adam and Eve sinned in the garden, everyone born after them was born into sin. The things that you do such as cursing, lying, smoking, drinking, fornicating etc., are the fruits of sin. When you are in darkness, it is your nature to sin. But, you must come out of darkness and into the marvelous light in order for the Holy Spirit to assist you in overcoming those sins through the Word of God.

The second step is to REPENT. According to *1 John 1:9*, if you confess your sins, God is faithful and just to forgive you of all your sins and cleanse you of all unrighteousness. Child of God, repentance is a change of heart, change of mind, and a change of direction. Meaning, you are going to make a 180-degree turn away from sin. If you made a 360-degree turn, you'll end up right back where you started. A Christian is not looking for a way to sin; he is looking for a way out of sin.

The third step is to CONFESS JESUS AS YOUR LORD AND SAVIOR. According to ***Romans 10:9-10***, that if we confess with our mouths and believe in our hearts that God raised Jesus from the dead, we shall be saved. You must speak this out loud. By speaking it out, you're renouncing Satan off the throne of your life, and placing Jesus as the head of your life.

If you would like to invite Jesus to be your Lord and Savior, now is the acceptable time. You can pray this prayer, and if you're really sincere about it, you will enter into a new life.

Deneen Whatley

Heavenly Father, I recognize that I am a sinner and I repent of my sins. Your Word says if I confess my sins, you are faithful and just to forgive me of my sins and cleanse me from all unrighteousness. Father God, You said in Your Word that anyone who confesses Your Son Jesus Christ, The Anointed One and His Anointing as Lord and Savior, and believes in his/her heart that You raised Him from the dead, will be saved. I believe that Jesus, the Anointed One is Your Son, and I acknowledge that He gave His blood at Calvary to pay for my sin, sickness, poverty and spiritual death. I renounce every work of darkness, and receive You now, Lord Jesus, as my personal Lord and Savior. According to Your Word, Lord, I'm now a new creation because I am in Christ. My past is dead and gone, and I have a new life in You. Thank You Lord Jesus, for exchanging the unrighteousness in my life for Your righteousness. I am the righteousness of God in You, Lord Jesus.

Now, believe Jesus is living in your heart. Jesus has forgiven you of your sins and made you righteous. Make a decision to obey the Word of God, and get into a church that teaches the Word of God with simplicity and understanding, so that you may apply it to your everyday life.

NOW, YOU ARE ON YOUR WAY TO HEAVEN! WELCOME INTO THE KINGDOM OF GOD!

Beloved,

"If you abide in My Word and My Word abides in you, then you are truly my disciplined one. And you will know the truth, and the truth will SET YOU FREE."

I'm looking forward to you writing me and letting me know you have accepted Jesus Christ as your Lord and Savior.

I would also like to know how this book has benefited you in your walk as a Christian.

Forever Serving Him!

Love Deneen

For more information about this ministry, to request a free brochure, or inquire about speaking engagements, please contact us at:

Deneen Whatley Ministries

P.O. Box 293042

Lewisville, Texas

Phone: (214) 884-9901

Please include your prayer requests

and testimony when you write.

ABOUT THE AUTHOR

Deneen Whatley resides in Lewisville, Texas with her wonderful husband, Eric and their amazing son, Chandler. She is a native of Dallas, Texas. Deneen has a genuine love for people and her most heartfelt desire is to see the will of God fulfilled in the lives of individuals who will allow God to be their priority.

In September 1993, she was inspired by God to establish a ministry for the purpose of teaching the Word of God in a way that will set people free from the yokes and bondages that entangle them. The Lord further informed her that this liberating ministry would be called, "Set Free Ministries, Inc."

In 2007, she founded Women Walking in the Word Int'l Ministries in Atlanta, Georgia. Women Walking in the Word Int'l Ministries is a women's outreach ministry focused and devoted to helping women heal from broken hearts as a result of life's situations and circumstances. For over 20 years she studied and served as a Minister under the leadership and direction of a mega church in College Park, Georgia.

Deneen is an international speaker, author, gospel artist, life coach and spiritual mentor to women all over the world.

Her first book, Greet Me With A Holy Kiss, was written and published in 1998. She is an international columnist operating under the moniker "Ms. Witty". Men and women have written to Ms. Witty for spiritual guidance with everyday questions and situations. Ms. Witty has been featured in numerous publications both domestically and abroad: The Graig Brooks Unity Newspaper in San Francisco, California, The Kingdom Times and the Building Builders publications in Nassau, Bahamas and Caicos Islands, the Gospel Bahamas Newspaper in the Exuma Islands, Bahamas and The Pensacola Voice (www.pensacolavoice.com) in Pensacola, Florida. Deneen has launched into both radio and television, hosting her own radio show, "The Reality of being Set Free Broadcast" at LOVE 860AM in Atlanta, Georgia. Additionally, she co-hosted a radio broadcast as Ms. Witty with DeShawn

Moore on MGM Radio in Fort Wayne, Indiana. She made her television appearance on Atlanta's WATC, Channel 57's broadcast," Atlanta Live". Your life will never be the same once you have experienced God's L.O.V.E. (Living, Overcoming, being Victorious, and Exceeding in the things of God) through Deneen Whatley's ministry!

God is truly awesome!

Write to her at writeme@mswitty.org "Ask Ms. Witty Anything" and she will be happy to answer you. Visit the website at www.mswitty.org.

www.ingramcontent.com/pod-product-compliance
Lightning Source LLC
Chambersburg PA
CBHW071140090426
42736CB00012B/2178